The Gentleman's
Devotional

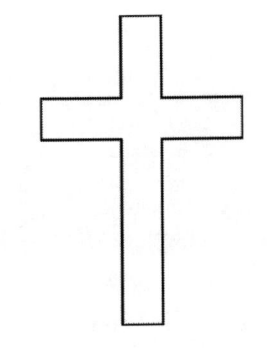

The Gentleman's Devotional

A Journey of Faith and Character

40 Day Devotional

Curtis Fabian

PRAIZE PRESS

www.praizepress.com

PRAIZE PRESS

Copyright © 2024 by Praize Press
All rights reserved.

No part of this book may be reproduced, distributed, or transmitted in any form or by any means, without the prior written permission of the publisher, except for brief quotations in a review or other non-commercial uses permitted by copyright law.

PRAIZE PRESS
info@praizepress.com

ISBN: 9798337742670

Printed in the United States of America
First Printing, 2024

Scripture Quotations

All Scripture quotations are taken from the King James Version (KJV) of the Bible, first published in 1611 under the authority of King James I of England. The KJV is in the public domain.

Images

All images included in this book are either in the public domain, licensed under CC0 (Creative Commons Zero), or similar license.

Dedication

First and foremost, I dedicate this book to my Lord and Savior, Jesus Christ, who has guided and sustained me through every step of this journey.

I also dedicate this book to George Heffelfinger, who played an instrumental role in my early years of studying scripture in depth. His influence and wisdom continue to shape my walk with the Lord. Though he is now with our Father in Heaven, his legacy lives on.

Finally, to you, the reader, thank you for taking the time to engage with this work. May it inspire and enrich your life as you walk the path of faith.

Table of Contents

Section 1: Foundations of a Gentleman

Day 1: The Power of Agape Love   11
Day 2: The Call to Honor   13
Day 3: Integrity in All Things   15
Day 4: Leading with Humility   17
Day 5: Cultivating Compassion   19
Day 6: Discipline in Action   21

Section 2: The Gentleman's Heart

Day 7: Guarding Your Heart   27
Day 8: Cultivating a Pure Heart   29
Day 9: A Heart of Compassion   31

Section 3: The Gentleman's Mind

Day 10: Renewing Your Mind   35
Day 11: The Power of Positive Thinking   37
Day 12: Cultivating Discernment   39
Day 13: Taking Every Thought Captive   41

Section 4: The Gentleman's Actions

Day 14: The Impact of Consistent Action   45
Day 15: The Power of a Good Example   47
Day 16: Serving Others with a Grateful Heart   49
Day 17: Overcoming Challenges with Faith   51

Section 5: The Gentleman's Relationships

Day 18: Building Strong Relationships   55
Day 19: Resolving Conflicts Peacefully   57

Day 20: A Husband's Duty: Lead like a Lion, Love like the Lamb   59
Day 21: Cultivating Empathy and Understanding   64
Day 22: Forgiving as Christ Forgave   66

Section 6: The Gentleman's Legacy

Day 23: Leaving a Lasting Impact   70
Day 24: Mentoring the Next Generation   72
Day 25: Building a Legacy of Faith   74
Day 26: Serving from a Place of Strength   76
Day 27: Evaluating and Reflecting on Your Legacy   78

Section 7: The Gentleman's Daily Walk

Day 28: Seeking God's Guidance   82
Day 29: Pursuing Righteousness   84
Day 30: Embracing God's Peace   86
Day 31: Living Out the Fruit of the Spirit   88
Day 32: Cultivating a Life of Gratitude   92
Day 33: Committing to Daily Prayer and Scripture   94

Section 8: The Gentleman's Influence in the World

Day 34: Influence Through Love   98
Day 35: Advocating for Justice   100
Day 36: Exemplifying Integrity in Your Work   102
Day 37: Being a Good Steward of Resources   104
Day 38: Engaging in Meaningful Service   106
Day 39: Living Out Christian Values   108
Day 40: Cultivating a Spirit of Generosity   110

The Journey of a Gentleman: End Reflection   113

Bonus Reflection: The Ego and God's Presence   115

Final Prayer & Dedication   117

Discussion Questions   118

Scripture Index   122

INTRODUCTION

Welcome to *The Gentleman's Devotional: A Journey of Faith and Character.*

This 40-day journey is designed to deepen your walk with God while helping you embody the virtues of a true gentleman. Each day presents a thoughtful reflection grounded in Scripture, practical guidance for daily living, and a prayer to guide your heart. As you navigate these pages, you'll discover ways to integrate honor, integrity, faith and more into every facet of your life.

This devotional is more than just a reading—it's a call to transform your character and impact the world around you in a meaningful way.

In a world where values are constantly tested, this devotional offers a steady compass, guiding you with confidence and grace. To enrich your experience, you'll find dedicated spaces for notes, encouraging you to reflect and personalize your journey. Jot down thoughts, prayers, or insights as you work through each day.

May each day bring you closer to the man God has called you to be, and may your journey through this book be filled with growth, inspiration, and a renewed commitment to living out your Christian faith.

Curtis Fabian

Section 1

Foundations of a Gentleman

Day 1

The Power of Agape Love

"Charity suffereth long, and is kind; charity envieth not; charity vaunteth not itself, is not puffed up, doth not behave itself unseemly, seeketh not her own, is not easily provoked, thinketh no evil; rejoiceth not in iniquity, but rejoiceth in the truth; beareth all things, believeth all things, hopeth all things, endureth all things." —1 Corinthians 13:4-7 (KJV)

Agape love is the highest form of love, a selfless, sacrificial love that transcends emotions and personal gain. It is the love that God has for humanity and the love He calls us to extend to others. Unlike conditional or transactional love, agape love is given freely, without expecting anything in return. It's the foundation of all other virtues and the hallmark of a true Christian gentleman.

Jesus demonstrated this perfect love through His life and sacrifice. He loved those who betrayed Him, healed those who doubted Him, and gave His life for those who rejected Him. This same agape love calls us to love not only those who love us back but also our enemies, the strangers we encounter, and those who cannot repay our kindness. It is a love that endures through trials, forgives without limits, and serves without seeking recognition.

For a gentleman, agape love is the foundation of all his relationships and interactions. It challenges us to see beyond our differences and to love others unconditionally, just as Christ loves us. How can you embody this kind of love? Begin by examining your motives. Do you love others with the expectation of something in return, or do you love them because Christ first loved you? Reflect on how you can show this pure, selfless love to those around you, even when it's difficult.

Agape love transforms not only our hearts but the hearts of those we touch. It creates a ripple effect, binding us together in unity and perfect harmony. Let this love be your guide today and every day.

Lord, fill me with Your agape love. Help me to love others as You have loved me—selflessly and sacrificially. May my love be a reflection of Your grace, and may it inspire others to know and experience the boundless love of Christ. Amen.

Today, find one person in your life whom you can love unconditionally. Show them agape love through a kind gesture, forgiving spirit, or selfless act. Let your actions reflect the perfect love that binds everything together in harmony.

DAY ONE NOTES

_____

_____

_____

_____

_____

Day 2

The Call to Honor

"And above all these things put on charity, which is the bond of perfectness." —Colossians 3:14 (KJV)

Honor is a fundamental virtue that defines a true gentleman. In a world where respect and reverence for others seem to be fading, a Christian man stands out by living a life marked by honor. But what does it mean to honor someone? In the biblical sense, honor goes beyond mere respect. It is an attitude of valuing others, recognizing their worth as created in the image of God, and treating them accordingly. Jesus exemplified honor in His interactions. He treated everyone—from the leper to the Pharisee—with dignity. He saw beyond the exterior and honored the image of God in each person.

For a gentleman, this means going beyond societal norms and choosing to honor others not based on their status or what they can offer but because they are beloved by God. How can you live out this call to honor? Begin by considering how you speak to and about others. Do your words uplift, or do they tear down? Are you quick to offer praise, or do you withhold it? As Romans 12:10 suggests, strive to outdo others in showing honor. This doesn't mean seeking to be better than others in a competitive sense but aiming to consistently lead in honoring others as Christ did.

Lord, help me to be a man of honor. Teach me to see others as You see them and to treat them with the respect and dignity they deserve. May my actions and words reflect the honor I have for You and for those You place in my life. Amen.

Identify one person in your life today whom you can honor in a special way. It could be a word of encouragement, a gesture of kindness, or simply showing gratitude. Make a conscious effort to outdo yourself in showing honor.

DAY TWO NOTES

_____

_____

_____

_____

_____

_____

_____

_____

_____

Day 3

Integrity in All Things

"He that walketh uprightly walketh surely: but he that perverteth his ways shall be known." —Proverbs 10:9 (KJV)

Integrity is the backbone of a gentleman's character. It is the quality of being honest and having strong moral principles, whether in public or in private. Integrity isn't just about avoiding lies or deceit; it's about living a life of transparency and trustworthiness in every situation. A man of integrity doesn't shift his values based on convenience or pressure but stands firm on the principles of God's Word.

Scripture is filled with examples of men who demonstrated integrity, even when it cost them dearly. Think of Daniel, who refused to defile himself with the king's food, or Joseph, who fled from Potiphar's wife, choosing imprisonment over sin. Their integrity was their security; it was the foundation of their trust in God.

In your own life, integrity means doing the right thing, even when no one is watching. It's easy to cut corners when you think no one will notice, but a gentleman understands that God always sees. Walking in integrity brings peace and security, knowing that your life is an open book before God and man.

> *Father, give me the strength to walk in integrity in every area of my life. Let my thoughts, words, and actions align with Your truth. Help me to be trustworthy and honest, reflecting Your character in all I do. Amen.*

Examine your life today for areas where you may be compromising your integrity. It could be in your work, relationships, or even in your private thoughts. Make a commitment to change, and ask God for the grace to live with integrity.

DAY THREE NOTES

_____

_____

_____

_____

_____

_____

_____

_____

_____

_____

_____

Day 4

Leading with Humility

"Let nothing be done through strife or vainglory; but in lowliness of mind let each esteem other better than themselves." —Philippians 2:3 (KJV)

Leadership and humility may seem like opposites, but in the kingdom of God, they are deeply intertwined. While worldly views often equate leadership with power and dominance, biblical leadership is rooted in servanthood and humility. Jesus, the ultimate example of a leader, demonstrated this by washing His disciples' feet—a task typically reserved for the lowest servant. Through this act, He showed that true leadership is not about being served, but about serving others.

A leader who embodies humility prioritizes the needs and well-being of others, not out of self-neglect but from a place of genuine respect and compassion. This approach does not imply that one's own needs and self-worth are disregarded. Rather, it means recognizing the value of others and acting with a spirit of empathy and service.

Maintaining a sense of self-worth while valuing others' needs involves balancing humility with self-care. It means leading with a heart that seeks to uplift and support others while also ensuring that one's own needs and boundaries are respected. Humility in leadership includes being open to admitting mistakes and seeking forgiveness, acknowledging that no position exempts one from accountability.

As you lead—whether in your home, workplace, or community—strive to reflect a heart of service and humility, glorifying God through your actions.

Lord Jesus, You are the ultimate example of humble leadership. Help me to lead with the same humility You demonstrated. Let my actions and decisions reflect a heart that is focused on serving others and glorifying You. Amen.

Identify a leadership role you hold—whether at work, in your family, or in your community. Today, look for ways to lead with humility, perhaps by serving those you lead in a practical way or by putting their needs before your own.

DAY FOUR NOTES

_____

_____

_____

_____

_____

_____

Day 5

Cultivating Compassion

"Finally, be ye all of one mind, having compassion one of another, love as brethren, be pitiful, be courteous:" —1 Peter 3:8 (KJV)

Compassion is the ability to empathize with others, to share in their joys and their sorrows, and to offer a hand of kindness in times of need. It's more than just feeling sorry for someone—it's the willingness to act in love and mercy. Compassion drives us to go beyond ourselves, to step into another's shoes, and to show Christ's love through tangible actions.

Jesus, throughout His ministry, exemplified compassion. He healed the sick, fed the hungry, and comforted the grieving. He wasn't moved solely by the crowd's needs but by their individual stories, their pain, and their humanity. His heart was always full of compassion, and it drove Him to act.

For a Christian gentleman, cultivating compassion means looking at the world through Christ's eyes. It's easy to become desensitized in a world filled with suffering and challenges, but God calls us to remain tender-hearted and responsive to the needs around us. Compassion requires us to slow down, to listen, and to care deeply.

How can you cultivate this Christ-like compassion? Begin by being present. Truly see the people in your life, their struggles, and their needs. Reach out to those who are hurting, even in small ways, whether through a kind word, a listening ear, or a helping hand.

Compassion is not just a feeling but a choice to act in love, to make someone's burden a little lighter.

Lord, help me to develop a compassionate heart. Open my eyes to the needs of those around me and give me the strength and grace to respond in love. May my compassion reflect Your mercy and be a beacon of hope to those who are hurting. Amen.

Identify one person today who is going through a difficult time. Reach out to them with an act of kindness or encouragement, offering a gesture of compassion that will remind them of Christ's love.

DAY FIVE NOTES

_____

_____

_____

_____

_____

_____

_____

Day 6

Discipline in Action

"Now no chastening for the present seemeth to be joyous, but grievous: nevertheless afterward it yieldeth the peaceable fruit of righteousness unto them which are exercised thereby." —Hebrews 12:11 (KJV)

Self-discipline is the cornerstone of spiritual growth and maturity. It involves more than simply being consistent—it's about having the inner strength to deny immediate gratification, to resist temptation, and to choose what aligns with God's will, even when it's uncomfortable or inconvenient. Biblically, discipline reflects God's shaping of our character, often through correction, challenges, and perseverance.

Discipline requires mastery over your desires, thoughts, and actions. In a world that constantly promotes indulgence and instant gratification, self-discipline calls you to a higher standard—one rooted in obedience to God. Hebrews 12:11 highlights that discipline, though often difficult and painful, leads to the peaceable fruit of righteousness. This fruit isn't just personal success or self-improvement; it's the outcome of a life conformed to Christ's example.

Jesus embodied perfect self-discipline. He fasted, prayed, and withdrew to quiet places to stay centered on the Father's will, even as He faced immense trials. His life shows us that self-discipline isn't about rigid control but about being in step with God's purpose. For a gentleman, self-discipline is the strength to prioritize godliness in every aspect of life, from how you manage your time, to how you respond to others, to how you handle temptation.

In practical terms, self-discipline begins with small but intentional steps. It's choosing to hold your tongue when anger rises, to pray when distractions abound, and to practice integrity even when no one is watching. Identify one area in your life where you feel pulled away from God's will. Whether it's in your thought life, habits, or relationships, commit to exercising self-discipline in that area. As you do, remember that self-discipline isn't about perfection, but about surrendering your desires to God, trusting Him to mold your character.

Lord, strengthen me with the discipline to deny my selfish desires and to align my life with Your will. Help me to exercise control over my thoughts and actions, to choose Your ways over my own, and to grow in righteousness each day. May my self-discipline reflect my devotion to You. Amen.

Today, choose one area where you need greater self-discipline. Over the next week, make deliberate decisions to act in accordance with God's will in that area. Trust Him to guide your efforts and grow you through the process.

DAY SIX NOTES

Conclusion of Section 1

In these first three days, you've laid the foundation for what it means to be a gentleman rooted in Christ. Honor, integrity, and humility are not just ideals to strive for but are the bedrock of a life that reflects the character of Jesus. As you continue this devotional journey, let these principles guide your thoughts, actions, and decisions, shaping you into the man God has called you to be.

END OF SECTION NOTES

_____

_____

_____

_____

_____

_____

_____

_____

Section 2
The Gentleman's Heart

Day 7

Guarding Your Heart

"Keep thy heart with all diligence; for out of it are the issues of life." —Proverbs 4:23 (KJV)

The heart is the seat of our emotions, desires, and will. It is the center of our being, from which all our thoughts, words, and actions flow. Proverbs 4:23 warns us to guard our hearts with all diligence because the condition of our heart determines the course of our life. A gentleman understands the importance of guarding his heart from anything that could corrupt or lead him astray.

Guarding your heart means being mindful of what you allow into your mind and soul. It involves filtering what you watch, listen to, and read, as well as who you spend your time with. It's about protecting your inner life from the influences of the world that can harden your heart or lead you away from God.

To guard your heart, you must be intentional about feeding it with the Word of God, prayer, and godly fellowship. A well-guarded heart is one that is rooted in Christ, continually nourished by His love, truth, and grace. When your heart is guarded, you are better equipped to navigate the challenges of life and to respond with wisdom and love.

Heavenly Father, help me to guard my heart with all diligence. Let Your Word be the filter through which everything passes, and may my heart be filled with Your love, truth, and grace. Protect me from the influences that seek to corrupt my heart and draw me away from You. Amen.

Take inventory of the things that influence your heart—what you watch, listen to, read, and the people you associate with. Make a conscious decision to remove or limit anything that is not beneficial to your spiritual well-being.

DAY SEVEN NOTES

_____

_____

_____

_____

_____

_____

_____

_____

_____

_____

Day 8

Cultivating a Pure Heart

"Blessed are the pure in heart: for they shall see God." — Matthew 5:8 (KJV)

Purity of heart is a hallmark of a true gentleman. A pure heart is one that is free from sin, hypocrisy, and deceit. It is a heart that seeks after God and desires to please Him in all things. Jesus Himself emphasized the importance of a pure heart, promising that the pure in heart will see God.

Purity isn't just about avoiding sin; it's about having a heart that is fully devoted to God. It's about your motives, thoughts, and desires aligning with His will. Cultivating a pure heart requires regular self-examination, repentance, and a commitment to holiness.

In a world filled with temptation and compromise, maintaining a pure heart is a daily battle. It means resisting the allure of sin and choosing to walk in righteousness. But the reward is great—intimacy with God and the ability to see Him clearly in your life.

> *Lord, create in me a clean heart and renew a right spirit within me. Help me to pursue purity in all areas of my life and to be free from anything that hinders my relationship with You. Let my heart be wholly devoted to You, and may I see You clearly as I walk in Your ways. Amen.*

Spend time in prayer today, asking God to reveal any areas of your heart that are not pure. Confess and repent of any sin, and ask the Holy Spirit to help you cultivate a heart that is pure and pleasing to God.

DAY EIGHT NOTES

_____

_____

_____

_____

_____

_____

_____

_____

_____

_____

_____

Day 9

A Heart of Compassion

"And be ye kind one to another, tenderhearted, forgiving one another, even as God for Christ's sake hath forgiven you." —Ephesians 4:32 (KJV)

Compassion is a defining characteristic of a gentleman. It is the ability to feel the pain of others and to be moved to act on their behalf. A heart of compassion is one that is tender, kind, and forgiving, reflecting the heart of God toward humanity.

Jesus was the ultimate example of compassion. He healed the sick, fed the hungry, and comforted the brokenhearted. His heart was always moved by the needs of those around Him, and He responded with love and care.

As His followers, we are called to do the same. A heart of compassion doesn't just feel sympathy for others; it moves you to action. It prompts you to reach out to those who are hurting, to offer a helping hand, and to show kindness and forgiveness, even when it's difficult. As a gentleman, your compassion should extend to everyone you meet, regardless of their background or circumstances.

Lord Jesus, fill my heart with Your compassion. Help me to be tenderhearted and kind, always ready to extend grace and forgiveness to others. Let my life be a reflection of Your love and compassion to those around me. Amen.

Look for an opportunity today to show compassion to someone in need. It could be a kind word, a helping hand, or simply being there for someone who is hurting. Let your actions be a reflection of the compassion of Christ.

DAY NINE NOTES

_____

_____

_____

_____

_____

_____

_____

_____

_____

_____

Conclusion of Section 2

The heart of a gentleman is one that is guarded, pure, and compassionate. These qualities are not just ideals to be admired but virtues to be cultivated daily. As you continue on this devotional journey, remember that the condition of your heart is vital to your walk with Christ. A well-tended heart will produce a life that honors God and blesses those around you.

End of Section NOTES

_____

_____

_____

_____

_____

_____

_____

_____

_____

Section 3

The Gentleman's Mind

Day 10

Renewing Your Mind

"And be not conformed to this world: but be ye transformed by the renewing of your mind, that ye may prove what is that good, and acceptable, and perfect, will of God." —Romans 12:2 (KJV)

The mind is the battlefield where spiritual battles are won or lost. The world constantly bombards us with messages that are contrary to God's Word, trying to conform our thinking to its ways. However, as a Christian gentleman, you are called to resist this conformity and instead be transformed by the renewing of your mind.

Renewing your mind involves aligning your thoughts with the truths of Scripture. It means rejecting worldly philosophies and embracing God's wisdom. This transformation is not a one-time event but a continuous process, requiring daily discipline and submission to the Holy Spirit.

The renewed mind is one that seeks to understand God's will in every situation. It discerns what is good, acceptable, and perfect according to God's standards, not the world's. When your mind is renewed, you are equipped to live a life that is pleasing to God, reflecting His character and fulfilling His purposes.

Heavenly Father, help me to renew my mind daily by Your Word. Let my thoughts be guided by Your truth, and may I resist the patterns of this world. Transform my mind so that I may understand and fulfill Your perfect will for my life. Amen

Set aside time each day to meditate on Scripture. Choose a verse or passage to reflect on throughout the day, asking God to renew your mind through His Word.

DAY TEN NOTES

_____

_____

_____

_____

_____

_____

_____

_____

_____

_____

Day 11

The Power of Positive Thinking

"Finally, brethren, whatsoever things are true, whatsoever things are honest, whatsoever things are just, whatsoever things are pure, whatsoever things are lovely, whatsoever things are of good report; if there be any virtue, and if there be any praise, think on these things." —Philippians 4:8 (KJV)

The thoughts you entertain have a profound impact on your life. Negative thoughts can lead to fear, anxiety, and discouragement, while positive, God-centered thoughts can bring peace, joy, and strength. Philippians 4:8 encourages you to focus your mind on what is true, honest, just, pure, lovely, and praiseworthy.

Positive thinking, in the biblical sense, isn't about denying reality or ignoring problems. Rather, it's about choosing to focus on the goodness of God, His promises, and the beauty of His creation, even in the midst of challenges. It's about filling your mind with thoughts that uplift and encourage rather than those that drag you down.

A gentleman understands the importance of guarding his mind against negativity. He actively chooses to dwell on thoughts that are in line with God's truth, knowing that what he thinks about will eventually influence how he feels and behaves. By focusing on positive, virtuous thoughts, you are setting the stage for a life marked by faith, hope, and love.

Lord, help me to focus my mind on what is good, true, and praiseworthy. Fill my thoughts with Your truth and let that truth guide my emotions and actions. May I be a man who thinks positively and reflects Your goodness in all I do. Amen.

When negative thoughts arise, counter them with Scripture. Memorize Philippians 4:8 and use it as a guide for your thoughts. Make a habit of replacing negativity with God's truth.

DAY ELEVEN NOTES

_____

_____

_____

_____

_____

_____

_____

_____

_____

_____

Day 12

Cultivating Discernment

"But strong meat belongeth to them that are of full age, even those who by reason of use have their senses exercised to discern both good and evil." —Hebrews 5:14 (KJV)

Discernment is the ability to judge well, to distinguish between good and evil, truth and error. It is a vital skill for any gentleman who desires to live a life that honors God. In a world filled with moral ambiguity and false teachings, discernment helps you navigate life's challenges with wisdom and integrity.

Hebrews 5:14 speaks of discernment as something that is developed over time through practice and maturity. It is likened to spiritual "meat" that is for those who are mature in their faith. Discernment is not merely an intellectual ability but a spiritual sensitivity that comes from a deep relationship with God and familiarity with His Word.

A gentleman exercises discernment by constantly seeking God's guidance and testing everything against Scripture. He does not simply accept what he hears but carefully evaluates it in light of God's truth. This discernment allows him to make wise decisions, avoid deception, and lead others in the path of righteousness.

> *Father, grant me the discernment to distinguish between truth and error, good and evil. Help me to grow in spiritual maturity so that I may exercise wise judgment in all areas of my life. May Your Word be the standard by which I measure all things. Amen.*

Commit to studying the Bible deeply and regularly, allowing God's Word to sharpen your discernment. When faced with a decision, ask for the Holy Spirit's guidance and compare your options with Scripture.

DAY TWELVE NOTES

Day 13

Taking Every Thought Captive

"Casting down imaginations, and every high thing that exalteth itself against the knowledge of God, and bringing into captivity every thought to the obedience of Christ." —2 Corinthians 10:5 (KJV)

Your thoughts have the power to shape your reality, and that's why it's crucial to take control of them. 2 Corinthians 10:5 challenges you to bring every thought into captivity to the obedience of Christ. This means not allowing your mind to wander into unhealthy or ungodly territory but instead, disciplining your thoughts to align with the mind of Christ.

Taking every thought captive involves being vigilant about what enters your mind. Thoughts that are rooted in fear, doubt, pride, or lust need to be identified and surrendered to Christ. It also means being proactive in filling your mind with godly thoughts, those that are in line with His will and character.

A gentleman understands that his thought life is directly connected to his spiritual life. He is aware of the influence his thoughts have on his behavior and his relationship with God. By taking every thought captive, you are actively participating in the transformation of your mind and the renewal of your spirit.

Lord, help me to take every thought captive to the obedience of Christ. Give me the strength to resist thoughts that are contrary to Your will, and fill my mind with thoughts that are pure, true, and pleasing to You. May my thought life reflect the mind of Christ in all things. Amen.

Monitor your thoughts throughout the day. When you notice a thought that is not in line with God's Word, immediately take it captive by confessing it to God and replacing it with a Scripture that speaks truth.

DAY THIRTEEN NOTES

_____

_____

_____

_____

_____

_____

_____

_____

_____

_____

Conclusion of Section 3

The mind of a gentleman is one that is renewed, positive, discerning, and disciplined. These qualities are not just beneficial for personal growth but are essential for living a life that honors God and influences others for His kingdom. As you continue your devotional journey, commit to cultivating a mind that reflects the wisdom and character of Christ.

END OF SECTION NOTES

_____

_____

_____

_____

_____

_____

_____

_____

Section 4

The Gentleman's Actions

Day 14

The Impact of Consistent Action

"And let us not be weary in well doing: for in due season we shall reap, if we faint not." —Galatians 6:9 (KJV)

Integrity isn't just a one-time act; it is a habit, a way of life. The true power of integrity lies in the consistency of our actions over time. Galatians 6:9 encourages us to persist in doing good, knowing that faithfulness in our actions leads to a fruitful outcome, even when the results aren't immediate.

In our walk as gentlemen, consistency in well-doing is key to building a life of honor and trustworthiness. Small, everyday decisions rooted in integrity build a legacy over time. When we remain steadfast in living out our faith, we become a reliable example to others, reflecting the character of Christ.

Every decision, every interaction is an opportunity to demonstrate the consistency of a life lived in alignment with God's truth. When challenges arise, it's the unwavering commitment to do what is right that marks a gentleman of integrity.

Lord, grant me the strength to be consistent in my actions. Help me not to grow weary in doing good, and remind me that, in Your time, I will see the fruit of my faithfulness. Amen.

How can you remain consistent in your actions, even when it feels discouraging? What small steps can you take today to demonstrate integrity in your daily life?

DAY FOURTEEN NOTES

_____

_____

_____

_____

_____

_____

_____

_____

_____

Day 15

The Power of a Good Example

"Let no man despise thy youth; but be thou an example of the believers, in word, in conversation, in charity, in spirit, in faith, in purity." —1 Timothy 4:12 (KJV)

Your actions serve as a powerful witness to others, especially to those who look up to you or observe your behavior. 1 Timothy 4:12 calls you to be an example to others in various aspects of your life: in your speech, conduct, love, faith, and purity. Your life should reflect the teachings of Christ and serve as a model for others to follow.

Being a good example means living out your faith consistently and visibly. It involves demonstrating Christian virtues in your daily interactions, whether in your work, relationships, or community involvement. Your example can inspire others to follow Christ and live according to His teachings.

A gentleman understands that his actions are a form of leadership. By setting a positive example, you influence others and help guide them toward a life that honors God. Strive to be a model of Christ-like behavior, knowing that your actions speak louder than words.

> *Heavenly Father, help me to be a good example to others in all aspects of my life. May my speech, actions, and attitude reflect Your love and truth. Guide me to live in a way that honors You and encourages others to follow Your ways. Amen.*

Consider the areas of your life where you can set a positive example for others. Take intentional steps to demonstrate Christ-like behavior, and seek feedback from trusted friends or mentors on how you can improve.

DAY FIFTEEN NOTES

_____

_____

_____

_____

_____

_____

_____

_____

_____

_____

_____

Day 16

Serving Others with a Grateful Heart

"But with the precious blood of Christ, as of a lamb without blemish and without spot:" —1 Peter 1:19 (KJV)

Service is a key component of living out your faith. 1 Peter 1:19 reminds us of the immense price Jesus paid for our salvation, highlighting the depth of His love and sacrifice. In response to this great gift, we are called to serve others with the same selfless love and gratitude. Serving others often involves putting their needs before your own and acting out of love and compassion. It can be expressed through acts of kindness, support, and generosity.

A gentleman understands that true service comes from a heart of gratitude for what Christ has done for him. Serving others not only meets their needs but also reflects your appreciation for Christ's sacrifice. It is a tangible way to show love and to live out the commands of Christ. By serving with a grateful heart, you honor God and demonstrate the transformative power of His love in your life.

Lord, help me to serve others with a heart full of gratitude for the sacrifice of Christ. Let my service be a reflection of Your love and grace, and may I be a blessing to those around me. Guide me to serve with humility and joy, knowing that I am honoring You through my actions. Amen.

Find an opportunity to serve someone in your community or church this week. Approach the task with a heart of gratitude, recognizing that your service is a response to the incredible love Christ has shown you.

DAY SIXTEEN NOTES

_____
_____
_____
_____
_____
_____
_____
_____
_____
_____

Day 17

Overcoming Challenges with Faith

"I can do all things through Christ which strengtheneth me." —Philippians 4:13 (KJV)

Challenges and difficulties are an inevitable part of life. However, Philippians 4:13 assures us that through Christ, we have the strength to overcome any obstacle. This verse is a reminder that our ability to face and conquer challenges is not based on our own strength but on Christ's power working in us.

A gentleman approaches challenges with a mindset of faith and reliance on God. Rather than being overwhelmed by difficulties, he seeks God's strength and guidance. By trusting in Christ's power, you can face trials with courage and resilience, knowing that you are not alone.

Overcoming challenges with faith involves maintaining a positive attitude, seeking God's help through prayer, and persevering despite setbacks. It's about seeing obstacles as opportunities for growth and trusting that God will use them for His purposes in your life.

> *Lord, I thank You for the strength You provide to overcome challenges. Help me to rely on Your power and not my own. Give me the courage and perseverance to face difficulties with faith, and use these challenges to grow me in Your grace. Amen*

Identify a current challenge you are facing and commit it to God in prayer. Seek His strength and guidance, and take practical steps to address the challenge with faith and perseverance.

DAY SEVENTEEN NOTES

Conclusion of Section 4

The actions of a gentleman—his integrity, example, service, and response to challenges—are crucial aspects of his Christian walk. Each action reflects his commitment to living out his faith and impacting those around him positively. As you continue to cultivate these qualities, remember that your actions are a testament to the transformative power of Christ in your life.

END OF SECTION NOTES

_____

_____

_____

_____

_____

_____

_____

_____

_____

Section 5

The Gentleman's Relationships

Day 18

Building Strong Relationships

"A friend loveth at all times, and a brother is born for adversity." —Proverbs 17:17 (KJV)

Relationships are a vital part of life, and building strong, lasting bonds is essential for a gentleman. Proverbs 17:17 highlights the nature of true friendship—one that is characterized by unwavering love and support, especially during times of trouble. A true friend is someone who remains loyal and loving regardless of circumstances.

Building strong relationships involves being present, supportive, and loving. It means investing time and effort into understanding and caring for others and being willing to stand by them through both good times and challenges. True friendship is not just about enjoying pleasant moments but also about being a source of strength and encouragement in difficult times.

For gentlemen, fostering strong male friendships is particularly important. Brotherhood provides a unique support network where men can share their struggles, seek counsel, and hold each other accountable. These friendships often become the backbone of one's faith walk, offering support, wisdom, and encouragement from peers who understand the challenges of a gentleman's journey.

As a gentleman, you are called to nurture and value relationships, whether with family, friends, or colleagues. Your relationships should reflect the love and commitment of Christ, demonstrating genuine care and reliability. In the context of male friendships, this means being a source of strength and encouragement to one another, actively investing in each other's spiritual and personal growth.

> *Lord, help me to build and maintain strong, loving relationships with those around me. Teach me to be a faithful friend and a supportive presence in times of need. May my relationships reflect Your love and grace. Amen.*

Reach out to a friend or family member you haven't connected with recently. Make an effort to strengthen the relationship by offering your support and letting them know you care.

DAY EIGHTTEEN NOTES

_____
_____
_____
_____
_____
_____
_____
_____

Day 19

Resolving Conflicts Peacefully

"If it be possible, as much as lieth in you, live peaceably with all men." —Romans 12:18 (KJV)

Conflict is a natural part of human relationships, but how you handle it can make a significant difference. Romans 12:18 encourages you to live peaceably with others as much as it depends on you.

This means actively working towards resolution and maintaining peace, even when disagreements arise. Resolving conflicts peacefully involves approaching the situation with a spirit of humility and a desire for reconciliation. It means listening to the other person's perspective, communicating openly and respectfully, and seeking common ground.

A gentleman understands the importance of preserving relationships and works diligently to address issues constructively. By handling conflicts with grace and a commitment to peace, you demonstrate the character of Christ and build stronger, more resilient relationships. Your approach to conflict can turn challenges into opportunities for growth and deeper understanding.

> *Heavenly Father, give me the wisdom and patience to resolve conflicts peacefully. Help me to approach disagreements with a spirit of humility and a desire for reconciliation. May my actions reflect Your peace and love. Amen.*

Identify a current conflict or tension in your relationships. Approach the situation with the intention of resolving it peacefully, using communication and understanding to address the issue.

DAY NINETEEN NOTES

_____

_____

_____

_____

_____

_____

_____

_____

_____

_____

_____

_____

_____

Day 20

A Husband's Duty: Lead like a Lion, Love like the Lamb

"Husbands, love your wives, even as Christ also loved the church, and gave himself for it;" —Ephesians 5:25 (KJV)

You are a husband because you chose her—because God placed a sacred mantle on your shoulders. You didn't stumble into this. You didn't marry for convenience or comfort. You accepted a divine call: to lead and love like Christ loves His Church.

This calling isn't about flowers or fleeting emotions—it's about the Cross. Christ bled for His bride, modeling the ultimate act of selfless love. That's your blueprint. You are to lead with strength and clarity, yet love with a heart willing to sacrifice—spiritually, emotionally, even physically—for her good.

As head of the household, your leadership must mirror His: strong, steady, and sacrificial. Not controlling. Not passive. You are a lion in battle—bold, protective, fearless. But you are also the lamb—gentle, humble, and willing to lay down your life.

"...that He might sanctify and cleanse it with the washing of water by the word."
— Ephesians 5:26

Your role is not to dominate—it's to sanctify. To wash her in the Word, not in your wounds. To guide her in holiness by the power of Scripture and the consistency of your example.

Don't become her emotional crutch. Become her spiritual covering.

"The head of the woman is the man... the head of every man is Christ."
— 1 Corinthians 11:3

You lead not by mood or merit, but by divine order. When she's overwhelmed, you don't drown with her—you anchor the home. You lead with resolve, not reaction. You're a man under authority, submitted first to Christ.

This leadership is not optional. It's not earned. It's appointed.

"You therefore must endure hardship as a good soldier of Jesus Christ." — 2 Timothy 2:3

Marriage isn't a battlefield of conflict—it's a battlefield to defend. And your wife? She's not your opponent. She's your assignment, your sacred trust, and your God-given partner in this war for holiness.

Roles of Husband and Wife in God's Order

God didn't design marriage as a competition—but a covenant. Husband and wife are equal in value, distinct in role, and united in purpose.

The husband is called to lead—not with pride, but with humility and love. *"Husbands, love your wives, just as Christ also loved the church and gave Himself for her."* — Ephesians 5:25

Biblical headship is not about privilege; it's about daily sacrifice—protecting, providing, guiding with patience and strength. A husband under God's authority leads by example, not entitlement.

The wife is called a helper—not in weakness, but in strength. The Hebrew word *"ezer"*—used of God Himself—means a strong support, a rescuer, a sustainer. *"Wives, submit to your own husbands, as to the Lord."* — Ephesians 5:22

This isn't inferiority. It's alignment under divine structure. When both husband and wife walk in obedience to their God-ordained roles, the home reflects heaven's order—and heaven's peace.

Biblical roles are not outdated. They are foundational.

Consecrate My Leadership, Lord

Father, sanctify my heart as a husband. Crush every ounce of laziness, selfishness, and pride in me. Replace my need for comfort with conviction. Teach me to lead my wife like Christ leads the Church—with truth, grace, sacrifice, and unwavering love. Help me love her soul more than her smile, to correct with gentleness, protect with strength, and provide with faith. When I fall short, convict me swiftly. Make me quick to repent and quicker to obey. Let my marriage be a testimony of Your order, Your holiness, and Your relentless love. In Jesus' mighty name, Amen.

Personal Reflection

Clean or Contaminate?

Are you washing your wife in the Word... or in your wounds?

Passive or Present?

Have you allowed emotional passivity to replace spiritual leadership?

Shepherd or Bystander?

When's the last time you prayed *with* her—not just *for* her?

Cover or Collapse?

When storms hit, do you anchor the home or add to the chaos?

Model or Mouthpiece?

Are you imitating Christ—or just talking about Him?

➲ Step up. Speak the Word. Lead without apology.

Reflection for Single Men – Prepare Like a King

You're not "waiting" for a wife—you're *becoming* a husband before she ever sees you.

Marriage doesn't make you a leader. Discipline does. Obedience to Christ *now* lays the foundation for how you will lead *then*. Stop fantasizing about a Proverbs 31 woman if you're not living like a Psalm 1 man.

- Are you in the Word daily?
- Are you leading yourself before asking God to trust you with someone else?
- Do you guard your purity like it matters to her soul—not just your pleasure?

If you can't steward your thoughts, your time, your body, or your habits—you are not ready to carry a crown or cover a bride. Be faithful with the field before asking for the garden.

Still, some men may be called to remain single—and this is not a lesser path. Paul wrote, *"It is good for a man not to marry"* (1 Corinthians 7:1), and later added, *"He who marries does well, but he who refrains from marriage will do even better"* (1 Corinthians 7:38). Singleness, when lived in devotion to the Lord, is a powerful and focused life. Whether called to marriage or to remain unmarried, the goal is the same: to live in full obedience to Christ.

DAY TWENTY NOTES

Day 21

Cultivating Empathy and Understanding

"Rejoice with them that do rejoice, and weep with them that weep." —Romans 12:15 (KJV)

Empathy is the ability to understand and share the feelings of others. Romans 12:15 calls you to rejoice with those who are happy and to weep with those who are sad. This verse underscores the importance of being emotionally present and supportive in your relationships.

Cultivating empathy involves actively listening to others, seeking to understand their experiences and emotions, and responding with compassion. It means celebrating others' successes and offering comfort during their struggles.

A gentleman demonstrates empathy by being attentive and responsive to the needs and feelings of those around him. By practicing empathy and understanding, you build deeper connections and create an environment where people feel valued and supported. Your ability to relate to others' emotions enhances your relationships and reflects the love of Christ.

> *Father, help me to cultivate empathy and understanding in my relationships. Teach me to rejoice with those who are happy and to offer support to those who are in need. May my interactions reflect Your compassion and grace. Amen.*

Identify someone in your life who may need emotional support. Reach out to them with a listening ear and offer your encouragement and understanding.

DAY TWENTY-ONE NOTES

Day 22

Forgiving as Christ Forgave

"Forbearing one another, and forgiving one another, if any man have a quarrel against any: even as Christ forgave you, so also do ye." —Colossians 3:13 (KJV)

Forgiveness is a central theme in the Christian faith, and Colossians 3:13 instructs you to forgive others just as Christ forgave you. Forgiveness involves letting go of resentment and choosing to release others from the debt they owe you because of their wrongs.

A gentleman practices forgiveness by acknowledging the hurt, choosing to forgive, and seeking reconciliation where possible. It means releasing grudges and extending grace, even when it is difficult.

By forgiving others, you mirror the forgiveness you have received from Christ, promoting healing and restoring relationships.

Forgiveness is not just an act but a continuous attitude that fosters peace and unity. It enables you to move forward from past hurts and maintain healthy, loving relationships.

Lord, help me to forgive others as You have forgiven me. Give me the strength to release grudges and to extend grace, even when it is difficult. May my heart be free from resentment and filled with Your love and peace. Amen.

Reflect on any unresolved conflicts or grudges you may have. Take steps to offer forgiveness, whether through a direct conversation or through a personal decision to release any lingering resentment.

DAY TWENTY-TWO NOTES

Conclusion of Section 5

The relationships of a gentleman are marked by love, respect, empathy, and forgiveness. Each aspect of this section emphasizes the importance of nurturing healthy and Christ-centered relationships. By investing in these relational qualities, you build stronger connections and reflect the character of Christ in your interactions with others.

END OF SECTION NOTES

Section 6

The Gentleman's Legacy

Day 23

Leaving a Lasting Impact

"A good man leaveth an inheritance to his children's children: and the wealth of the sinner is laid up for the just." —Proverbs 13:22 (KJV)

Leaving a lasting impact involves more than just providing material wealth; it encompasses the values, principles, and spiritual legacy you pass on to future generations. Proverbs 13:22 emphasizes that a good man leaves an inheritance not just for his children but for his grandchildren, highlighting the importance of a legacy that endures beyond one's lifetime.

A gentleman's legacy is built on the principles he lives by and the example he sets. It includes the way he influences his family, the contributions he makes to his community, and the values he imparts. This impact is often seen in how others remember him and the positive changes his life has fostered.

Creating a meaningful legacy requires intentional living. Consider how your actions and decisions today will affect those who come after you. Strive to build a legacy of faith, integrity, and love that will inspire and guide future generations.

> *Lord, help me to live in a way that leaves a lasting, positive impact on those around me. Guide me to build a legacy of faith, integrity, and love that will benefit future generations. May my life be a testament to Your grace and truth. Amen.*

Reflect on the legacy you wish to leave behind. Identify steps you can take to ensure that your life reflects your values and principles, and actively work towards building a meaningful impact on those around you.

DAY TWENTY-THREE NOTES

Day 24

Mentoring the Next Generation

"The things that thou hast heard of me among many witnesses, the same commit thou to faithful men, who shall be able to teach others also." —2 Timothy 2:2 (KJV)

Mentoring involves sharing your wisdom, experience, and faith with others, particularly those who are younger or less experienced. 2 Timothy 2:2 highlights the importance of passing on what you have learned to others who can continue to teach and impact future generations.

As a gentleman, mentoring provides an opportunity to invest in others and help them grow in their faith and character. It involves guiding, encouraging, and supporting others as they navigate their own journeys. Effective mentoring is rooted in genuine care and a commitment to seeing others succeed and flourish. Mentoring can take many forms, from formal programs to informal relationships.

Consider how you can be a mentor to someone in your community, church, or family. Your guidance and support can make a significant difference in their lives and contribute to a positive, lasting legacy.

Father, guide me in my efforts to mentor and support others. Help me to share my wisdom and experience in a way that encourages and empowers them. May my mentoring relationships reflect Your love and help others grow in their faith and character. Amen.

Identify someone you could mentor or support. Reach out to them and offer your guidance and encouragement, committing to invest in their growth and development.

DAY TWENTY-FOUR NOTES

Day 25

Building a Legacy of Faith

"And these words, which I command thee this day, shall be in thine heart: And thou shalt teach them diligently unto thy children, and shalt talk of them when thou sittest in thine house, and when thou walkest by the way, and when thou liest down, and when thou risest up." —Deuteronomy 6:6-7 (KJV)

Building a legacy of faith involves instilling the teachings and values of Christianity in those around you. Deuteronomy 6:6-7 emphasizes the importance of keeping God's commandments in your heart and teaching them diligently to your children. This ongoing process includes discussing and living out these teachings in everyday situations.

A gentleman's legacy of faith is reflected in how he nurtures his own spiritual growth and guides others in their faith journey. It involves setting an example of devotion, prayer, and obedience, and making faith a central part of daily life.

To build a legacy of faith, integrate spiritual practices into your family routines, personal habits, and community involvement. Your commitment to living out and teaching your faith will leave a lasting impression on those around you and impact future generations.

Lord, help me to build a strong legacy of faith. May Your Word be deeply rooted in my heart, and guide me to teach and model Your principles in all aspects of my life. May my faith impact those around me and inspire future generations. Amen.

Find ways to incorporate spiritual teachings into your daily life and interactions with others. Consider creating family or personal traditions that emphasize the importance of faith and pass these practices on to future generations.

DAY TWENTY-FIVE NOTES

_____

_____

_____

_____

_____

_____

_____

_____

_____

_____

Day 26

Serving from a Place of Strength

"Thou shalt love thy neighbour as thyself."—Matthew 22:39 (KJV)

A meaningful legacy is built on impactful actions and values. Effective service to others comes from a place of personal strength and renewal. Just as Jesus commanded us to love our neighbors as ourselves, it's crucial to remember that serving others effectively begins with caring for our own well-being. By maintaining this balance, we ensure that our actions remain fruitful and that our legacy is one of thoughtful, sustained impact.

Imagine a candle that lights the way for others. If the candle burns too quickly without being replenished, it will extinguish before it has fulfilled its purpose. Similarly, our service to others requires us to maintain our own spiritual, emotional, and physical health. By loving ourselves through self-care and spiritual nourishment, we can continue to offer love and support to those around us without depleting ourselves.

Heavenly Father, thank You for the command to love our neighbors as ourselves. Help us understand that to serve others well, we must care for our own well-being. Grant us wisdom to balance self-care with our acts of service and strength to love others from a place of renewal. May our service reflect Your love and grace, and may we seek refreshment in Your presence. In Jesus' name, Amen.

Today, remember that loving your neighbor as yourself involves recognizing your own needs for rest, reflection, and renewal. As you serve others, make sure to take time to refresh your own spirit and body. This balance will enable you to serve from a place of strength and compassion.

DAY TWENTY-SIX NOTES

Day 27

Evaluating and Reflecting on Your Legacy

"So teach us to number our days, that we may apply our hearts unto wisdom." —Psalm 90:12 (KJV)

Evaluating and reflecting on your legacy involves assessing how you have lived and what impact you have made. Psalm 90:12 encourages us to be mindful of our days and to apply our hearts to wisdom. This reflection helps you understand the direction of your life and the legacy you are building.

Taking time to evaluate your legacy means considering how your actions align with your values and goals. Reflect on the ways you have influenced others, contributed to your community, and lived out your faith. This process helps you make necessary adjustments and focus on areas that will enhance your legacy.

Regular reflection ensures that you are intentional about your actions and their long-term impact. By being thoughtful about your legacy, you can make meaningful changes and continue to build a legacy that honors God and benefits others.

Lord, help me to reflect on my life and my legacy with wisdom and clarity. Show me areas where I can grow and make a positive impact. Guide me to live intentionally and to leave a legacy that honors You and serves others. Amen.

Set aside time for reflection on your life and legacy. Assess how your actions align with your values and goals, and identify any areas where you can make changes to enhance your impact.

DAY TWENTY-SEVEN NOTES

_____

_____

_____

_____

_____

_____

_____

_____

_____

_____

_____

_____

_____

Conclusion of Section 6

The legacy of a gentleman is shaped by his faith, actions, and influence on others. By focusing on leaving a lasting impact, mentoring others, building a legacy of faith, practicing generosity and service, and reflecting on your life, you create a legacy that honors God and positively affects future generations.

END OF SECTION NOTES

_____

_____

_____

_____

_____

_____

_____

_____

_____

_____

Section 7

The Gentleman's Daily Walk

Day 28
Seeking God's Guidance

"I will instruct thee and teach thee in the way which thou shalt go: I will guide thee with mine eye." -- Psalm 32:8 (KJV)

Embracing God's guidance is essential for navigating the complexities of life and walking faithfully. Psalm 32:8 promises that God will provide direction and instruction for those who seek Him. Understanding and following God's guidance helps us align our actions with His will and ensures we remain on the right path.

Consider areas in your life where you may need clearer guidance or direction. How can you more actively seek and follow God's leading in these areas?

Lord, thank You for Your promise to guide me and instruct me in the way I should go. Help me to listen to Your voice and trust in Your direction. Teach me to seek Your wisdom and follow Your leading in every aspect of my life. Amen.

This week, make a conscious effort to seek God's guidance in your decisions. Commit to regular prayer and Bible study to align your actions with His will.

DAY TWENTY-EIGHT NOTES

Day 29

Pursuing Righteousness

"But seek ye first the kingdom of God, and his righteousness; and all these things shall be added unto you." —Matthew 6:33 (KJV)

Pursuing righteousness means prioritizing God's kingdom and His ways above all else. Matthew 6:33 instructs you to seek the kingdom of God and His righteousness first, with the promise that all other needs will be met. Righteousness involves living in accordance with God's will and reflecting His character in your daily actions.

A gentleman dedicated to righteousness actively seeks to align his life with biblical principles, making choices that honor God and benefit others. This pursuit shapes your character and decisions, influencing how you interact with the world and handle challenges. By focusing on righteousness, you invite God's blessings and direction into your life.

Heavenly Father, help me to seek Your kingdom and righteousness above all else. Guide my actions and decisions to reflect Your will and character. Thank You for Your promise to meet my needs as I pursue You. Amen.

Evaluate your priorities and daily activities. Make adjustments to ensure that seeking God's kingdom and righteousness is at the forefront of your life.

DAY TWENTY-NINE NOTES

Day 30

Embracing God's Peace

"And the peace of God, which passeth all understanding, shall keep your hearts and minds through Christ Jesus." — Philippians 4:7 (KJV)

Embracing God's peace involves allowing His peace to guard your heart and mind, even in challenging circumstances. Philippians 4:7 promises that God's peace, which surpasses all understanding, will keep you secure in Christ. This peace is not dependent on external situations but is a deep, internal assurance provided by God.

A gentleman who embraces God's peace remains calm and steady, regardless of life's ups and downs. This peace helps you navigate stress, anxiety, and difficulties with a sense of security and trust in God's plan. Embracing this peace enables you to respond to situations with grace and confidence.

Lord, grant me Your peace that surpasses all understanding. Help me to embrace this peace in all circumstances and to trust in Your plan and provision. May Your peace guard my heart and mind in Christ Jesus. Amen.

Identify any areas of stress or anxiety in your life. Practice letting go of these worries and trusting in God's peace by spending time in prayer and meditation on His promises.

DAY THIRTY NOTES

Day 31

Living Out the Fruit of the Spirit

"But the fruit of the Spirit is love, joy, peace, longsuffering, gentleness, goodness, faith, Meekness, temperance: against such there is no law." —Galatians 5:22-23 (KJV)

Living out the fruit of the Spirit means manifesting the qualities described in Galatians 5:22-23 in your daily life. These attributes—love, joy, peace, longsuffering, gentleness, goodness, faith, meekness, and temperance—reflect the character of Christ and are evidence of the Holy Spirit's work within you.

A gentleman guided by the fruit of the Spirit exhibits these qualities consistently, impacting those around him positively. Living out these attributes involves intentionality and reliance on the Holy Spirit's guidance, enabling you to embody Christ's character in your interactions and decisions.

The Fruit of the Spirit Defined and Lived Out

Love – Love is the selfless, sacrificial, and unconditional care for others.

> Put others before yourself by showing kindness and compassion, even when it's challenging. Love demands action—sacrificing time, energy, and resources to serve those around you.

Joy – Joy is a deep, abiding sense of gladness that comes from knowing God, independent of circumstances.

> Focus on God's goodness to cultivate joy, even during tough times. Rejoice in His presence and promises, while spreading encouragement to those around you.

Peace – Peace is a state of tranquility and contentment that comes from trusting God.

> When faced with conflict or anxiety, rest in God's sovereignty. Strive to be a peacemaker, resolving conflicts in a way that reflects Christ's heart.

Longsuffering (Patience) – Patience is the ability to endure difficult situations and people with a calm and forgiving heart.

> In frustrating circumstances, stay calm and composed, extending grace to others. Trust in God's perfect timing through all challenges.

Gentleness – Gentleness is the quality of being kind, tender, and compassionate in your actions and words.

> Speak and act thoughtfully, considering the feelings of others. Gentleness diffuses tension and reflects Christ's humility in all interactions.

Goodness – Goodness is moral excellence, the desire to do what is right and just.

> Uphold integrity by doing what is right, even when unnoticed. Actively seek ways to bless others through kindness and justice.

Faith (Faithfulness) – Faithfulness is steadfast loyalty and trustworthiness, both to God and others.

> Be consistent in your commitments and relationships. Build trust by keeping your word and staying faithful to God, even in difficult times.

Meekness – Meekness is strength under control; it's humility and submission to God's will.

> Lead with humility, recognizing your strength comes from God. Use that strength not for pride but to serve others with grace and humility.

Temperance (Self-control) – Self-control is the ability to master your desires, emotions, and actions.

> Exercise discipline in all areas of life. Whether in your speech, habits, or responses, practice self-restraint to reflect Christ's influence over your choices.

> *Father, help me to live out the fruit of the Spirit in all areas of my life. May love, joy, peace, and the other qualities described in Galatians 5 be evident in my actions and interactions. Guide me to reflect Your character in all I do. Amen.*

Choose one fruit of the Spirit to focus on for the day. Look for opportunities to practice this quality in your interactions with others and reflect on how it impacts your relationships and decisions.

DAY THIRTY-ONE NOTES

Day 32

Cultivating a Life of Gratitude

"In every thing give thanks: for this is the will of God in Christ Jesus concerning you." —1 Thessalonians 5:18 (KJV)

Cultivating a life of gratitude involves recognizing and appreciating the blessings and provisions of God in every aspect of your life. 1 Thessalonians 5:18 instructs you to give thanks in everything, as this reflects God's will for you in Christ Jesus. Gratitude shifts your focus from what is lacking to what is present and good.

A gentleman who cultivates gratitude maintains a positive perspective, even amidst difficulties. This attitude of thankfulness fosters contentment and joy, influencing how you approach life's challenges and blessings. By regularly expressing gratitude, you acknowledge God's goodness and provision, enhancing your overall well-being.

Lord, help me to cultivate a heart of gratitude in all circumstances. Teach me to give thanks for Your blessings and to recognize Your provision in every aspect of my life. May my gratitude reflect Your goodness and grace. Amen.

Start a gratitude journal. Each day, write down three things you are thankful for and reflect on how these blessings impact your life. Make it a daily habit to express gratitude in your prayers and interactions.

DAY THIRTY-TWO NOTES

Day 33

Committing to Daily Prayer and Scripture

"But we will give ourselves continually to prayer, and to the ministry of the word." —Acts 6:4 (KJV)

Committing to daily prayer and Scripture involves dedicating time each day to communicate with God and immerse yourself in His Word. Acts 6:4 emphasizes the importance of continual devotion to prayer and the ministry of the Word. This commitment helps you stay spiritually focused and nurtures your relationship with God.

A gentleman who prioritizes daily prayer and Scripture engagement finds strength, guidance, and encouragement. Regular prayer and study deepen your understanding of God's will and equip you to live out your faith with purpose and clarity.

Heavenly Father, help me to commit to daily prayer and the study of Your Word. Guide me in my time with You, and let it strengthen my faith and relationship with You. May my daily practices reflect a genuine devotion to Your will. Amen.

Establish a daily routine for prayer and Bible study. Set aside a specific time each day to read Scripture and pray, and stick to this commitment consistently. Consider using a Bible reading plan or devotional guide to enhance your study.

DAY THIRTY-THREE NOTES

Conclusion of Section 7

The daily walk of a gentleman is characterized by humility, righteousness, peace, the fruit of the Spirit, gratitude, and a commitment to prayer and Scripture. By integrating these practices into your daily life, you cultivate a Christ-centered approach to living that influences your actions, interactions, and overall character.

END OF SECTION NOTES

_____

_____

_____

_____

_____

_____

_____

_____

_____

Section 8
The Gentleman's Influence in the World

Day 34

Influence Through Love

"And now abideth faith, hope, charity, these three; but the greatest of these is charity."— 1 Corinthians 13:13 (KJV)

As a Christian gentleman, your influence in the world is not defined by wealth, status, or personal achievements but by how well you live out the love of Christ. Faith and hope are vital—they anchor your trust in God and keep you steadfast through trials. But love, or charity, is what the world truly notices. It's not just a feeling but an action, a deliberate choice to place others before yourself. When you act out of love, you reflect the character of Christ, making your influence more meaningful and lasting.

In a world often driven by self-interest, love stands out as countercultural. A gentleman who leads with love is a rare and valuable presence. People will remember your kindness, your patience, and your willingness to serve, more than any words you say or deeds you accomplish. This kind of love—charity—isn't always easy. It requires sacrifice and sometimes means putting others' needs ahead of your own comfort. But it's through these acts of selfless love that your influence as a man of God truly begins to shape the world around you.

Love isn't just the greatest of the three virtues; it's the greatest way to influence others for Christ. A heart filled with charity transforms how you engage with the world, from your personal relationships to your role in your community. People are drawn to the authenticity of love, and through that love, they are drawn closer to God. As you navigate your daily walk, remember that the most impactful thing you can do is love others well, for in doing so, you bring the Kingdom of God nearer to them.

Father, help me to be a man whose influence is shaped by love. Let the love of Christ flow through me as I interact with the world, and may my life reflect the selfless, enduring charity that brings glory to You. Amen.

Look for a way to influence someone today through a quiet, loving action—whether offering encouragement, showing mercy, or lending a helping hand. Let your love be your strongest influence.

DAY THIRTY-FOUR NOTES

_____

_____

_____

_____

_____

_____

_____

Day 35

Advocating for Justice

"Learn to do well; seek judgment, relieve the oppressed, judge the fatherless, plead for the widow." —Isaiah 1:17 (KJV)

Advocating for justice involves standing up for the rights of the oppressed and vulnerable. Isaiah 1:17 calls you to seek justice, relieve oppression, and advocate for those in need. This reflects God's heart for justice and righteousness.

A gentleman who advocates for justice actively seeks to address inequalities and support those who cannot advocate for themselves. This includes being informed about social issues, supporting fair practices, and using your influence to promote positive change. Your advocacy should reflect the love and justice of God in tangible ways.

Father, guide me in advocating for justice and supporting those in need. Help me to act with compassion and courage, standing up for what is right and making a positive impact in the world. Amen.

Research a local or global issue related to justice and find a way to get involved. This might include volunteering, supporting organizations that work for justice, or raising awareness about the issue.

DAY THIRTY-FIVE NOTES

Day 36

Exemplifying Integrity in Your Work

"And whatsoever ye do, do it heartily, as to the Lord, and not unto men." —Colossians 3:23 (KJV)

Exemplifying integrity in your work goes beyond meeting expectations or following company policy. Colossians 3:23 reminds us that the ultimate measure of our work is how we serve the Lord in all that we do. A gentleman who works heartily with integrity is motivated by a higher calling—pleasing God rather than simply gaining the approval of others. This means conducting yourself with honesty, diligence, and commitment to excellence, regardless of who is watching or what the situation demands.

Integrity at work isn't just about avoiding dishonesty but ensuring that every task, no matter how small, reflects your commitment to doing what is right in God's eyes. When you approach your work with this mindset, you honor God and become a witness to His grace and truth in a professional setting.

Lord, help me work heartily for You, displaying integrity in all I do. Let my efforts reflect Your righteousness, and may I serve You with excellence and honesty in every task. Amen.

Reflect on how your current work practices align with the standard set in Colossians 3:23. Are you working as though for the Lord? Identify one area where you can raise your standards of integrity and dedicate yourself to doing everything with a sincere heart.

DAY THIRTY-SIX NOTES

Day 37

Being a Good Steward of Resources

"Moreover it is required in stewards, that a man be found faithful." —1 Corinthians 4:2 (KJV)

Being a good steward of resources involves managing what you have —time, money, and talents—with faithfulness and responsibility. 1 Corinthians 4:2 emphasizes that stewards must be found faithful, reflecting the importance of responsible management.

A gentleman who is a good steward uses his resources wisely and generously, recognizing that everything ultimately belongs to God. This includes budgeting carefully, investing in meaningful causes, and using your talents to benefit others. Stewardship is a practical expression of your faithfulness and commitment to God's purposes.

Father, help me to be a good steward of the resources You have entrusted to me. Guide me in managing my time, money, and talents faithfully, and help me use them to honor You and serve others. Amen.

Assess your current stewardship practices and set goals for improvement. Create a plan to manage your resources more effectively, ensuring that you are using them in ways that honor God and benefit others.

DAY THIRTY-SEVEN NOTES

Day 38

Engaging in Meaningful Service

"And whosoever will be chief among you, let him be your servant." —Matthew 20:27 (KJV)

Engaging in meaningful service means prioritizing the needs of others and serving with a heart of humility and dedication. Matthew 20:27 teaches that true leadership is marked by servanthood, reflecting Christ's example.

A gentleman who engages in meaningful service actively seeks opportunities to serve others selflessly, whether through volunteer work, mentorship, or acts of kindness.

This type of service not only benefits those you help but also aligns with Christ's call to serve as He did. By dedicating your time and efforts to the well-being of others, you demonstrate a commitment to making a positive impact in the world and embody the essence of true Christian leadership.

Lord, inspire me to engage in meaningful service that reflects Your love and humility. Help me to seek opportunities to serve others and to make a positive difference in their lives. Amen.

Identify a specific service project or opportunity to volunteer for. Commit to participating and contributing your time and efforts to make a meaningful impact in your community.

DAY THIRTY-EIGHT NOTES

Day 39

Living Out Christian Values

"Let your light so shine before men, that they may see your good works, and glorify your Father which is in heaven."
—Matthew 5:16 (KJV)

Living out Christian values isn't about seeking recognition or applause but about reflecting Christ in everything you do. Matthew 5:16 encourages you to let your light shine—not for personal glory, but so that others may see God's goodness and glorify Him. This kind of living means embodying your faith through humility, kindness, and consistency, allowing your actions to point others toward God, not yourself.

A gentleman who truly lets his light shine does so in quiet, everyday ways that naturally flow from his love for God. Whether it's helping others, speaking truth with grace, or serving faithfully without seeking attention, the goal is always to honor the Lord. Your life should serve as a beacon of God's love, compassion, and righteousness, drawing people to Him through how you live, not through a desire to be seen.

Father, help me to live out my Christian values with humility, letting my actions speak of Your grace and love. May everything I do bring glory to You and inspire others to seek You. Amen.

Consider how your daily actions reflect your faith. Look for opportunities to serve or share the love of Christ in ways that don't seek recognition but point others toward God. Let your focus be on honoring Him, not on being seen by others.

DAY THIRTY-NINE NOTES

_____

_____

_____

_____

_____

_____

_____

_____

_____

_____

_____

_____

Day 40

Cultivating a Spirit of Generosity

"Give, and it shall be given unto you; good measure, pressed down, and shaken together, and running over, shall men give into your bosom. For with the same measure that ye mete withal it shall be measured to you again." —Luke 6:38 (KJV)

Cultivating a spirit of generosity means being open-handed with your resources and willing to bless others without expecting anything in return. Luke 6:38 promises that generosity will be reciprocated, often in greater measure than what you give.

A gentleman who cultivates generosity seeks opportunities to share his resources, time, and talents with others. This spirit of giving reflects the heart of God and fosters a culture of kindness and support. Generosity enriches both the giver and the receiver, demonstrating the transformative power of Christ's love.

Lord, cultivate in me a spirit of generosity. Help me to give freely and abundantly, trusting in Your provision and reflecting Your love through my actions. May my generosity be a blessing to others and honor You. Amen.

Identify an area where you can be more generous. Whether through financial support, giving your time, or offering your skills, make a plan to give generously and see how it impacts those around you.

DAY FORTY NOTES

Conclusion of Section 8

The gentleman's influence in the world is characterized by being a light, advocating for justice, exemplifying integrity, managing resources faithfully, engaging in service, living out values publicly, and cultivating generosity. By embracing these principles, you make a positive impact on the world around you and reflect Christ's character in your daily life.

END OF SECTION NOTES

_____

_____

_____

_____

_____

_____

_____

_____

_____

_____

The Journey of a Gentleman

End of Book Reflection: Embracing Purpose, Growth, and a Life Well Lived

---

As you conclude *The Gentleman's Devotional*, take a moment to reflect on the journey you've traveled. This 40-day experience was designed to deepen your Christian walk and develop the character of a true gentleman. It's not just a devotional; it's a call to live with purpose, grow in faith, and impact the world around you.

Embrace Your Purpose
Colossians 3:23 reminds us to do all things as if for the Lord. Whatever your passions or talents, when aligned with God's will, they become acts of worship. Psalm 37:4 reminds us that when we find joy in the Lord, He aligns our desires with His purpose, guiding us towards a meaningful path. Reflect on how your passions can serve God's kingdom and the greater good. Just as Jesus transformed Peter's fishing skills into a mission for bringing others to Christ, consider how your talents can be used to advance God's work.

Commit to Growth
Your spiritual growth is a lifelong journey. Philippians 1:6 assures us that God, who began a good work in you, will continue to perfect it. Celebrate the progress you've made and set new goals

for deepening your faith. Remember, growth is ongoing, and each day presents new opportunities to learn and draw closer to Christ.

Live as a Beacon of Light

Matthew 5:16 calls us to let our light shine before others, reflecting Christ's love and grace. Every action, word, and decision is a chance to glorify God. Whether through acts of kindness, serving others, or simply living with integrity, let your life be a testament to His work in you.

A Prayer for the Journey

> *"Lord, thank You for the growth and lessons You've given me through this journey. Help me to use my passions and talents to serve You and others. Guide me as I continue to grow in faith, and may my life always reflect Your light. Amen."*

As you move forward, continue to set spiritual goals, serve with your talents, and shine the light of Christ in all you do.

Bonus Reflection

The Ego and God's Presence

Understanding the Ego's Role

In the journey of a gentleman living out Christian values, it's important to recognize the role of the ego. The ego often represents our drive for self-promotion, control, and validation. It's the part of us that seeks approval and significance from the world. However, when we place our trust and focus solely on ourselves, we risk missing out on the deeper fulfillment and identity that comes from a relationship with God.

How God Replaces the Ego

The presence of God in our lives offers a transformative shift. When we make room for God, we allow His love and grace to define our worth and guide our actions. This is echoed in Galatians 2:20: "I am crucified with Christ: nevertheless I live; yet not I, but Christ liveth in me." As we center our lives on God, the ego's need for validation and control diminishes. We no longer need to seek validation through self-promotion because our identity and worth are anchored in Christ.

Living Out This Transformation

Embracing this shift involves daily surrender and trust in God's plan. Proverbs 3:5-6 reminds us: "Trust in the Lord with all your heart, and lean not on your own understanding; in all your ways acknowledge Him, and He shall direct your paths." By releasing the ego and relying on God, we find strength and direction that go beyond our own efforts.

Final Reflection

As you reflect on the teachings of this devotional, consider how you can apply these insights to your life. How might letting God replace the ego's influence help you live more fully in accordance with your Christian values?

Heavenly Father, we thank you for guiding us through this devotional journey. Help us to let go of the ego's demands and fully embrace our identity in You. May our lives reflect Your love and grace, and may we find our worth and purpose in Your presence alone. Amen.

Final Prayer and Dedication

*Heavenly Father, We come before You with gratitude for the lessons learned throughout this devotional. We thank You for guiding us as we strive to live lives marked by faith and character. We dedicate ourselves to Your service, seeking to embody these principles in every aspect of our lives. Help us to be men of character, whose actions reflect Your love and truth. May we honor others, lead with humility, and remain steadfast in our faith. Strengthen us to overcome challenges, resist temptation, and live with a clear perspective on Your eternal promises. As we move forward, we commit ourselves to growing in these virtues and to leaving a lasting legacy that glorifies You. Empower us to make a positive impact in our families, communities, and the world, always reflecting the light of Christ. In Jesus' name, we pray.
Amen.*

Discussion Questions

Foundations of a Gentleman

Honor and Integrity

- What does honor mean to you, and how do you define it in your daily life?
- Can you think of a recent situation where you had to choose between taking the easy way out and acting with integrity? How did you handle it?
- How does living a life of honor set you apart as a Christian gentleman in today's society?

Humility and Leadership

- How can humility make you a better leader?
- What areas of your life do you struggle to show humility, and why do you think that is?
- Jesus exemplified servant leadership. What are some practical ways you can lead with humility in your home, workplace, or community?

Guarding the Heart

- What do you think it means to "guard your heart"?
- What habits or influences could be putting your heart at risk, and how can you address them?
- Proverbs 4:23 reminds us to guard our hearts because everything we do flows from it. How does this apply to the way you interact with others?

Discussion Questions

The Gentleman's Heart and Mind

Renewing the Mind

- Romans 12:2 speaks of the importance of renewing the mind. In what areas of your life do you need to transform your thinking to align more closely with God's will?
- How can you be more intentional about filling your mind with things that are good, true, and honorable?
- What are some of the common lies or negative thoughts that take root in your mind, and how can you replace them with God's truth?

Compassion and Empathy

- Why is it important for a Christian gentleman to cultivate a compassionate heart?
- How do you show empathy in your relationships, and where could you improve?
- Jesus showed compassion to all, regardless of their status or background. How can you better reflect this same attitude in your daily interactions?

Living Out the Fruit of the Spirit

- Which of the fruits of the Spirit do you find the easiest to live out, and which do you struggle with the most?
- In what ways can you be more intentional about practicing the fruit of love, joy, peace, patience, and kindness in your life?
- How can demonstrating these qualities influence the people around you, especially those who may not share your faith?

Discussion Questions

Actions and Relationships

The Power of Example

- Who has been the most influential example of a Christian gentleman in your life? What did you learn from them?
- How can you be a better example of Christ's love to your family, friends, and community?
- Reflect on a time when your actions might not have aligned with your values. What steps can you take to be more consistent?

Building Relationships

- What are some ways you can build stronger, more meaningful relationships with those around you?
- How can you demonstrate love and respect to those with whom you disagree, particularly in a divided world?
- How does leading with empathy and understanding impact your ability to resolve conflicts peacefully?

Discussion Questions
Legacy and Influence

Leaving a Lasting Impact

- What kind of legacy do you want to leave behind, both spiritually and relationally?
- Are there areas in your life where you feel your actions and values aren't leaving the legacy you hope for? What changes can you make?
- How can you be more intentional about mentoring others and passing on your faith to the next generation?

Being a Light in the World

- How can you let your light shine more brightly in your workplace, community, or family?
- What does it look like to live out your Christian values in a public setting? How do you handle opposition or criticism when doing so?
- In what ways can you engage in meaningful service to those around you, reflecting Christ's love to a broken world?

Committing to Ongoing Growth

- As this devotional journey ends, what practices can you commit to in order to keep growing as a Christian gentleman?
- Are there areas of your life that require further spiritual maturity? How can you pursue growth in those areas?
- What steps will you take to hold yourself accountable to living out the values and lessons you've learned?

Scripture Index

DAY 1

1 Corinthians 13:4-7 (KJV)

"Charity suffereth long, and is kind; charity envieth not; charity vaunteth not itself, is not puffed up, doth not behave itself unseemly, seeketh not her own, is not easily provoked, thinketh no evil; rejoiceth not in iniquity, but rejoiceth in the truth; beareth all things, believeth all things, hopeth all things, endureth all things."

DAY 2

Colossians 3:14 (KJV)

"And above all these things put on charity, which is the bond of perfectness."

DAY 3

Proverbs 10:9 (KJV)

"He that walketh uprightly walketh surely: but he that perverteth his ways shall be known."

DAY 4

Philippians 2:3 (KJV)

"Let nothing be done through strife or vainglory; but in lowliness of mind let each esteem other better than themselves."

DAY 5

1 Peter 3:8 (KJV)

"Finally, be ye all of one mind, having compassion one of another, love as brethren, be pitiful, be courteous:"

Scripture Index

DAY 6
Hebrews 12:11 (KJV)

"Now no chastening for the present seemeth to be joyous, but grievous: nevertheless afterward it yieldeth the peaceable fruit of righteousness unto them which are exercised thereby."

DAY 7
Proverbs 4:23 (KJV)

"Keep thy heart with all diligence; for out of it are the issues of life."

DAY 8
Matthew 5:8 (KJV)

"Blessed are the pure in heart: for they shall see God."

DAY 9
Ephesians 4:32 (KJV)

"And be ye kind one to another, tenderhearted, forgiving one another, even as God for Christ's sake hath forgiven you."

DAY 10
Romans 12:2 (KJV)

"And be not conformed to this world: but be ye transformed by the renewing of your mind, that ye may prove what is that good, and acceptable, and perfect, will of God."

DAY 11
Philippians 4:8 (KJV)

"Finally, brethren, whatsoever things are true, whatsoever things are honest, whatsoever things are just, whatsoever things are pure, whatsoever things are lovely, whatsoever things are of good report; if there be any virtue, and if there be any praise, think on these things."

Scripture Index

DAY 12

Hebrews 5:14 (KJV)

"But strong meat belongeth to them that are of full age, even those who by reason of use have their senses exercised to discern both good and evil."

DAY 13

2 Corinthians 10:5 (KJV)

"Casting down imaginations, and every high thing that exalteth itself against the knowledge of God, and bringing into captivity every thought to the obedience of Christ."

DAY 14

Galatians 6:9 (KJV)

"And let us not be weary in well doing: for in due season we shall reap, if we faint not."

DAY 15

1 Timothy 4:12 (KJV)

"Let no man despise thy youth; but be thou an example of the believers, in word, in conversation, in charity, in spirit, in faith, in purity."

DAY 16

1 Peter 1:19 (KJV)

"But with the precious blood of Christ, as of a lamb without blemish and without spot:"

DAY 17

Philippians 4:13 (KJV)

"I can do all things through Christ which strengtheneth me."

Scripture Index

DAY 18

Proverbs 17:17 (KJV)

"A friend loveth at all times, and a brother is born for adversity."

DAY 19

Romans 12:18 (KJV)

"If it be possible, as much as lieth in you, live peaceably with all men."

DAY 20

Ephesians 5:25 (KJV)

"Husbands, love your wives, even as Christ also loved the church, and gave himself for it;"

Peter 3:7; 1 Corinthians 11:3

DAY 21

Romans 12:15 (KJV)

"Rejoice with them that do rejoice, and weep with them that weep."

DAY 22

Colossians 3:13 (KJV)

"Forbearing one another, and forgiving one another, if any man have a quarrel against any: even as Christ forgave you, so also do ye."

DAY 23

Proverbs 13:22 (KJV)

"A good man leaveth an inheritance to his children's children: and the wealth of the sinner is laid up for the just."

Scripture Index

DAY 24

2 Timothy 2:2 (KJV)

"And the things that thou hast heard of me among many witnesses, the same commit thou to faithful men, who shall be able to teach others also."

DAY 25

Deuteronomy 6:6-7 (KJV)

"And these words, which I command thee this day, shall be in thine heart: And thou shalt teach them diligently unto thy children, and shalt talk of them when thou sittest in thine house, and when thou walkest by the way, and when thou liest down, and when thou risest up."

DAY 26

Matthew 22:39 (KJV)

"Thou shalt love thy neighbour as thyself."

DAY 27

Psalm 90:12 (KJV)

"So teach us to number our days, that we may apply our hearts unto wisdom."

DAY 28

Psalm 32:8 (KJV)

"I will instruct thee and teach thee in the way which thou shalt go: I will guide thee with mine eye."

DAY 29

Matthew 6:33 (KJV)

"But seek ye first the kingdom of God, and his righteousness; and all these things shall be added unto you."

Scripture Index

DAY 30

Philippians 4:7 (KJV)

"And the peace of God, which passeth all understanding, shall keep your hearts and minds through Christ Jesus."

DAY 31

Galatians 5:22-23 (KJV)

"But the fruit of the Spirit is love, joy, peace, longsuffering, gentleness, goodness, faith, Meekness, temperance: against such there is no law."

DAY 32

1 Thessalonians 5:18 (KJV)

"In every thing give thanks: for this is the will of God in Christ Jesus concerning you."

DAY 33

Acts 6:4 (KJV)

"But we will give ourselves continually to prayer, and to the ministry of the word."

DAY 34

1 Corinthians 13:13 (KJV)

"And now abideth faith, hope, charity, these three; but the greatest of these is charity."

DAY 35

Isaiah 1:17 (KJV)

"Learn to do well; seek judgment, relieve the oppressed, judge the fatherless, plead for the widow."

Scripture Index

DAY 36

Colossians 3:23 (KJV)

"And whatsoever ye do, do it heartily, as to the Lord, and not unto men."

DAY 37

1 Corinthians 4:2 (KJV)

"Moreover it is required in stewards, that a man be found faithful."

DAY 38

Matthew 20:27 (KJV)

"And whosoever will be chief among you, let him be your servant."

DAY 39

Psalm 37:4 (KJV)

"Delight thyself also in the Lord: and he shall give thee the desires of thine heart."

DAY 40

Luke 6:38 (KJV)

"Give, and it shall be given unto you; good measure, pressed down, and shaken together, and running over, shall men give into your bosom. For with the same measure that ye mete withal it shall be measured to you again."

Scripture Index

JOURNEY REFLECTION

Colossians 3:23 (KJV)
"And whatsoever ye do, do it heartily, as to the Lord, and not unto men."

Psalm 37:4 (KJV)
"Delight thyself also in the Lord: and he shall give thee the desires of thine heart."

Matthew 5:16 (KJV)
"Let your light so shine before men, that they may see your good works, and glorify your Father which is in heaven."

BONUS REFLECTION

Galatians 2:20 (KJV)
"I am crucified with Christ: nevertheless I live; yet not I, but Christ liveth in me."

NOTES

NOTES

NOTES

NOTES

ISBN: 9798337742670

Made in the USA
Columbia, SC
19 June 2025